knowledge
in the
hands

HEATHER BROWNE PRINCE

GOOSE LANE

Published with the assistance of the New Brunswick Department of Municipalities, Culture and Housing and the Canada Council, 1994.

Cover photograph by Dale McBride.
Book design by Julie Scriver.
Printed and bound in Canada by The Tribune Press.
10 9 8 7 6 5 4 3 2

Canadian Cataloguing in Publication Data

Prince, Heather Browne
  Knowledge in the hands

  ISBN 0-86492-180-2

I. Title.

PS8581.R56K66 1994   C811'.54   C94-950066-6
PR9199.3.P75K66 1994

Goose Lane Editions   7/12/95
469 King Street
Fredericton, New Brunswick
Canada E3B 1E5

in memory of
Laura Adair
Samuel Brown

Contents

Desk-Talk

Not ideas about the thing but the thing itself.
— *Wallace Stevens*

The Thing is the loudest before it takes its bow —
A wall with one strip of paper curling down
Is the wall most blank, most straight, most wall.

And the key not on the table is the one regarded.
The purse over the vacated chair
Within the empty room the richest, the blackest purse.

How deeply we reach down into the various pockets
For dimes, asking directions to the rooms where we
Expect a response from the walls. We demand the walls to speak.

For a dime we want the place to give up its secrets.
It is, we say, our due for being here.
On the wall there is no time for incongruity.
Have you not straightened pictures?

The Thing rides the tongue, part stranger, part poem
Inside these walls it sounds where
Knuckles wooden and days get hollowed out.

Annabelle Hydrangea

I am becoming fairly familiar with Annabelle —
Last fall I hacked back her limbs and this spring
again in my rubber boots I tend to her,
Trenching the ground water to the city mains.

She trembles where I splash about
She revolts, sticks her sticks in my hair and eyes,
Racking the shovel that carries away her doubleness.

This summer she will rival the stars and
Transform northern girls into Tahitian Women:
>the pink bloom behind their ear
>the first hint of twilight turning
>their hands violet and warm
>suffusing his face

For Annabelle I dig a trench and dizzy myself
Beating back water snakes.
I would not have you see this:
I would colour your vision so that:
Turning away you will remember only:
A woman, like any other, irrigating
In black rubber boots her city lot.
>Tending, perennial.

Anniversary Request

I really don't want roses this year.
Roses fall and weep red-eyed
And I have to tend to them,
To their twelve disciple-heads
And the longing in their green leaves.
Oh   please
Don't give me roses.
They die so easily in spite of me
Their red pinched faces widen and waste.
Oh, please, roses are meant for some other
        place,
For someone who can dismiss roses easily
Tossing them aside when they begin to pout.
My books are speckled with the remnants of
        roses.
Oh, please listen,
"There is no room in this house
for even one doubting rose."

Back Talk

Your back is the rock where I mouth
Ribbed lines, and kiss the keeled leaf,

Draw and place my tied lips in the small
Sweet foaling sweep, bury my busied ear.

I lie there reached. My arms wrapped beyond the face,
Tying us to this revolving space with hands.

I imagine the core absorbing wet words.
I wait in warmth for sleep.

The wave trowels up   slips into relief
Sands   brackets   slithers   keeps
All angularity dissolved

The bone is dissolved
All the openings are closed save the navel

And a slight singular breathing in the breast camped down,
A breathing out of season
Sweet breath of sheets
The windows rattling down their dog-throated notes.

Window Poem

small flitting bird
tatted in the lilac;
small fluttered heart
behind the slats
of a blind;
your heart's beat
is also mine.

Image on Highway

Poised on a rise
of road the grouse stood
still and sharp as a bait hook
turned side to,
a simple shape
within the stroke and slash
of page-wire shadowing.
"A partridge," he said too quick.
                    "No, don't," she asked too late.

        Stopped
the feathers fed out beneath the Buick
like November leaves tumbling over and over.

The trunk slammed.

Tamarack limbs spread strangely bare
between them and the wet-gray stare
of the Washademoak   They drove
(his fingers sticky to wheel and blood, blood and wheel)
        She listened
for movement   in the back
        a final flutter

                            a wing   beat

by a herd of cows he found occasion to speak:
"Polled," he said
(the cows stared back at them)
"Their horns will never grow." And because
(she supposed) the fields were dying
he could not add
that
one of the nicest things he knew
was a fenced field of green
black with Angus

Stilled
she felt the image
formed and tugging at her eyes.

within the blood

           the loon's cry.
From a black lake
inane rhythms repeat,

mutilate

           the soundings
of loons
calling
           for what is felt,
             what is felt

over wires, and filaments
that now cause the light to bend

our call is removed
           from our voices

voices obfuscating.

on the lake the white
ringed eye
mistresses a field
most black.

inane rhythms,
            no answers

the blood
repeats.

Loon

If by chance you give God His right name, you will make Him God in truth, and on creating Him you will create yourself.

— *Miguel de Unamuno*

Over this lake
over this place
and in the headbones
she circles   and truth escapes

from her sides
from her wings
from the word she wreathes —
        loon.

        One tap and an anvil shears off —
            One tap and magnetism is displaced —
                One word and the world is

in the headbones   the word aches
        over this place
            over this place

Grieving his wife

he holds the shovel that laid back the earth,
the naked burial of light underneath.

He spills a shovelful of earth over the bulbs.
And works the brown earth as he had her breasts

in the day's light, between his fingers. The bulbs

half-grieved of the ground: this spring impatient
for life. For days with rain, with sun. Eager to

burst their own soft sides. In his eyes, green spears.
The shovelful of earth to keep from going blind.

You Ask Me What I Am Afraid Of

You ask me what I am afraid of here in your house.
The answer is simple: the way your collar presses
against your hair; the width of your wrists.

I don't tell you this, or of my fear of men who hold
out their fingers like roosts.
Of words flying between us, night swallows.

(They tie a woman's hands so she won't tear herself.
Up on the birthing bed she rips
the air with her mouth.)

And I am afraid of the strength in you gathering me down
pulling me up; of your hands, my words
coming hard and endless into the belly, out of the womb.

Going Where I Touch

Going where the barn cannot be taken by the wind.
Where my father sets into grooves a plank twenty by five
against the doors; secures a latch to the door's screw-eye
        and tests
the length and the strength of wood.

Where the small door's braced with a peavey and a stone.
Where my father tells of a wind that took the roofs;
Where he banks the coals with ashes to save the flue;
        bows
when he fills the cat's bowl with warmed milk.

Going, I double-check for the axe, the wrench and the spare
full on its rim.　The jack.　My old coat
(the flashlight deep in its pocket).
        I am
my father's daughter going back. I check the things I pack.

Going back where we pull to the doors on ropes, and he says,
"The brooks are riled." While we work the doors
he says that the clouds are braiding up. Being where the words close
and hook
I say: "There isn't a wind that can take her."

Here is the Smell of Smoke

Here is the smell of smoke
and the grunt of shadows. On the walls
beautiful women speak in their skin,
long-haired and ivory-mouthed.

Here the tapered ashen end of burning:

snow broken from its bough
pillowed to the ground. Light hovers at a doorway:
light at the mouth of the cave seen from within.

Here I tease a small flame with a stick. Ashes
lie on the surface of my arms.
A flame lifts its body
along the bodies of women painted on your wall.
Naked and full. Lying and standing.

Here is the smell of smoke and burned skin.

I squat over my heels and tend
to this burned spot on your floor. My hips
throw grotesque shadows of their own.

I suck on stone.

My eyes are wild and large.
My toes are spread, beautiful bones.

I go back. My eyes fall back, white skulls,
to the time of horny tongue and barbels,
back to the savage mute line across the face —
to a stoned mouthing,
to the rock depth of my hand
rubbing against a wall.

Light
heightens each of our bones. Mine
and these women painted on your wall.

One creeping flame lifts.

Here the smell of burning and scorched skin.
Ash, the body of our hands.
The long red line draws down the arm:
longer than hatred. Harder,
your hands on my head.

The Beginning of Sight

I met you before the saints came
to build walls for our tribe to graze behind
like cattle. Clipping the wild thyme in their teeth.

I met you before ships spread beyond the Hebrides,
before their mastheads and rigging tendrilled our shore, clung
wrecked on rock. I knew you when we breathed into fire-pots.

When we lit the hills in Erin with our breath.
When we broke the necks of sea grasses,
made our drink. When we leaned back into the earth,

into the fields. Into the faces of god in the field.
I knew you when we gathered close, our tribe
close, our horses close, our thighs close. Our hearts

closer than brooched cloaks when our voices rubbed sides;
when our hands soothed animal hides like water;
when your hands spoke to me like words. When fire hung

from reeds at our waist. Welled in our hands. When palms
illumined the sight. When we disturbed the air with ashes.
In ash the footsteps, bracken, and singed hair.

You and I descending the hills red-eyed as the Ancients.
With sooted hands, stares. With blackened teeth.
I met you when there were only the hands,
before there were ever the walls to hold us in.

Until A Promise is Fulfilled

There is the public
and the private poem,
and this, by its text,
is public, and can't reflect
its center, the nearer it gets
to the meadow it must lie down;
there, meets the openness and stands
upon the palm of the land.
There in quiet respect
it meets the neglect
of abandoned farm land —
there, takes by the hand
the ancient working hand
piling rock upon rock
until a promise is fulfilled —
and the world recedes a little
here and there alders flame;
an old apple tree staggers;
again the fever for fields,
for something cleared, begins —
and in it, the private poem.

The Apparition / The Field

Someone stole in, leaving flowers.
Like doves in the hall they cooed
in the dark, their song shed from soft
full throats. Like a seed their name.

Their petals opened into the night, red
as old drapery, romantic poetry, mauve
as the cloak of Christ bleeding at dusk
into an outcropping of rock. In the fields

Goldenrod and stalks of Indian tobacco;
the rustling heads of paperwhite.
The sun burns in each; each, in its singular voice,
is heard.

Silence

silence so soft
you touch
the sides of it with your mind. So low
in the dove-moan of evenfall, you want
to go down with it into the earth, sealed.

Sealing your lips to its lips as cool
and dark as a hidden spring,
its form flattened to the water drunk
as an animal on four splayed legs.
A woman drinks in silence
where she returns as a child returns
to the beckoning scarecrow,
where she listens to the song of oats
in the wind, the held call of the sun;
to the sheets whitening
and tugged by the long shadows in any back yard.
As a child to the eaves heavy with rain
and the nesting bodies of birds turning within.

Second Invocation

Brigit, I call.
Brigit, daughter of Dagda, sister to Bodb Derg;
sister to Aengus Mac-in-Org;
Brigit, the pagan, whose namesake
became Christ's in Kildare:

Brigit, I call.

Brigit, who left the print of her foot
in the ashes of the hearth;

who wandered by the walls,
who wailed by the cairns; who lit this world

as the underworld with gems, light, gold.
Brigit, who followed day's light

into the even, the light piercing the sight of the eye
in order for the heart to see.

In the heart a fire's dance. On the far hill
the wolves lament, the wolves abiding

so that the piper might lift from the ground
the sorrow. For an ogham, an inscription

in a bit of aspen for my lip's
chanting; I call for a bird to keep the pot from boiling

as long as the bird is in it. Brigit
for an anklet, a diadem, a gold thumb-ring;

for a time of rings under an old sun;
an old sky. Brigit, the horse and rider straddled

between this side and the other.

The Fire Place

1

You show me, brother, the fieldstones
their true faces
turned to the outside of the fireplace
their roughness turned in.

Your fingers measure
  appreciative
   &
  apprehensive
the depth of the thread of mortar
holding the rocks.

The fireplace a central thought
in this room
holding the memory of rocks
an examination of the earth
turned up and over and out
of ancient rockwalls,
dug from the girth
of cellars and set up here
made into perfect locks of colour:

pyrite up their sleeves,
green forests in their facets,
their inner secrets
irregularly revealed.
They stare back at you
where you look at them rising up
two storeys   to reappear amongst trees
perfectly heady   cured of the ground.

2

What moves you
to lug home so many
terrible stones from the fields, brother, & lay
them out in patterns about
your home?
Making constellations. Lodes of stones
arranged and rearranged
until
their still forms reveal
the glitter in their faces
and their original propensity
to be
stone.

What moves you, brother, to explicate
a form out of
such pieces
what bright particular
do you seek
to first set down, and which piece do you pick
next, each after each?

What logic is there
in the building of
a fire place?
The creation fixed,
lodged at the center,
not easily pronounced
by the heft or the moving
settling-down
of   stone   but
realized only in the cold home
of stone.
　　A reflection
of an old burning —
a peculiarity of itself.

3

Whatever it was
waits
like star-fire
infinitely peaceful and at war
        (a wooden bowl turned upside down
        looks a lot like heaven).
Across your sky of floor, brother,
the cold burnings roll —
a thick warehouse of earth.
Blocks, reclaimed by you,
to climb back up
into heaven   breathing
your name
into the dome. They say
that you were as they
for a time:
solid
and with purpose.

My Father's Ostlers

That Christmas Eve, he left the family
for a place where we couldn't follow.
From his chair, my father for hours
sat and stared, nudged in like a colt
to its mother's side. Waiting there
for someone to come. For someone to reach
that great distance over his old head
and hand him the lead with the brass star.

It was, I believe, his own father who came —
he was the only one able to answer
his need to ride out of there, the only one
old enough and wise enough to release
the harness from the nail on the crossbeam.
The only one to leave him go free.
The colt was coaxed from the barn
and my father's eyes filled with tears.

His voice skittered and shied
and he cried out for all of us to hear:
Watch out, watch out, my dears.

We are my father's ostlers.
We keep watch and whisper into the ears
of several beasts drawing near. We ask
childish questions. We ask: What brought
us here, and what is to be borne?

My mother's hand

because Ginsberg said to meditate
on those things that save
the poet from her fucking ideas —
my mother's hand, small, strong
as sand. My hand dazzling in her hand —
　　　so bright, too soon, too quick —
Ginsberg, what comes after this?

A White Gift

this soil not only between
but within
my fingers, a part of
the very cells that shape this poem.
                              — *Alden Nowlan*

Oh remember
In your narrowing dark hours
That more things move
Than blood in the heart.
                              — *Louise Bogan*

Seeking something yet unfound, though I have
    diligently sought it many a long year,
Singing the true song of the soul fitful at random,
Renascent with grossest Nature or among
    animals . . .
                              — *Walt Whitman*

Making gestures for myself I live
only occasionally
breaking through the surface of things
as they seem.

In the barn thought is held in beams.
In the barn my grandfather watches the light,
says it's time
to be getting in.

From over his head he plucks an egg;
out of the chaff, in the shafts of barn-light —
a white gift for me. He rubs it on his sleeve.
And winks.

It is my grandmother's voice I hear.
From the seams of a golden floor
where dreams hide in the daytime she
breasts her voice. And in the chimes.
And each time I set down a spoon.

At this time of morning there is no fire in the sky,
no orange ball rising above the trees, and in this dark
no grain spills in the half-light, in the corn-light.

I wait in this place.

There is no end to this place;
or to the soft cooing of the bird
dusting itself like a wild thing.
In the rafters, birds.

And the light spilling itself into yet
another room.

Were I that easy motion streaming
and bled from the beams, or showing
copper light at the edge, or smoothed in bottles
set down on the dusty ledge of this place.

Were I real,
and not the reflection caught within an eye;
were you the dark moth brushing my face.

There is magic in the arc of a man's hands
wherein he describes the curve of a bridge.

I am a woman. I squat over my knees

bending the light of the body, I make

difficult the posture of being.   Of loving.

My body folds into the clasping of your hands.

My cloth is gesture.

My eyes are nervous. Your words are everywhere.

Your words are wings
pinioned to my center.

If you are the dark moth, brush my face:
your hands rest. With the idle stasis of a moth's wings.
Their soft darkness
and their regret.

I conjure your hands lifting.
Making gestures for myself I live
only occasionally
breaking through the surface of things
as they seem.

Your hands rest. I watch them
softly open
and close down.

Sometimes they enfold
my own.

Once in a vacant room
where the sunlight fell, bright spoons on a golden floor.
And once, in the loam smells of a barn
where a rodent swelled under the straw.

From empty rooms I have heard the sounds

of her concertina closing down forty years.
She held it, a brown goose against her breast,
and sang its belly on her lap. And laughed.

There is no end to this place. No end to the mirrors
on these walls. Mirrors, you tell me, are old
as time.
   Time is an egg in my grandfather's hand —
   Birds, I say, can sometimes fly up into mirrors,
remain there: a stigmata of wings and beaks.
   I say this into your eyes

hoping that you can see.

In the barns chaff is suspended.
Thought is held in beams.
Days end with a tinkling of bells.
Or with her chimes stirring in the maples.
Her instrument lowing inside of rooms.

Time is an egg in my grandfather's hand.
   A white gift.

The men in my life have held their hands.
They've had stolid ones that do not fly up
as yours do, taking the air, describing this space
between us.

They held tight to the bowls
when the women were near. They did not pour
their tea into saucers. Their eyes were large and wary,
their temples beat like teaspoons against the cup.

Your talk stops when your hand falls
from the air. I hear a clattering of spoons.

Words are not ours
in public rooms.

Looking out of a glass
there's nowhere to go.

Making gestures from myself I live
only occasionally
breaking through the surface of things . . .

Once in a vacant room
sunlight fell in spoons.

I wear my hands in my pockets.
I am not unlike the men in my life in this.

There is the soft coo.

In the rafters the dusting.

There is an integrity in the barn.
In all things that remain   that wait.

Old wheels, the spokes broken, keep
distances within an arching of wood.

You tell me of one you carry with you.
Calling her by name when you grow afraid:
when you hear the birds you cannot see;
when birds move web-like over your face.

Bottles on sills glow. In the half-light
of this place we watch for corn-light, carry it with us
as much as anything
may be
ushered

from one place to another.

From one memory to the next.

When I trip and fall into walls
along the length of wainscoting leading,
within the old glass falling and beading,
I take your hand and say: Haven't we met before?

What is seen in the other?

What makes the eyes shy, turn away?

What stills the memory, says, "No, it can't be."

We say that this is a mistaking,
this knowledge in the hands.

At the tips of the fingers, the remembering.

In their fluttering,
                     wings.

In the barn the things that remain.

The buckwheat in the black bin.
The buckwheat shaped like stars.

First there is a dark sky.
Then a white moon, then a red sun.

Some things return and reach.
Arms and the supplication of arms
reach and return
for the end, for the lost ends.

For things dropped,

lost

and rolling.

Under the straw

shadow.

Under the pale wood of the stanchions
the necks that rubbed, the tongues that spoke
of hay, water, and more.

Under the crossbeams
and in the basin turned upside down,
forgotten. In the hair snagged on the door,
in the awful weight of doors pushed open
into the yard. In the pecking white hen.

Under the straw —

is this where we end,

is this where we end weeping
at the sight of birds?

There has been a death.

Birds are feeding
on my arms.
Are tangled in my hair.

Wood absorbs the voice.
Wood binds to wood. To sills.
Thresholds and rafters. The body stills.
Waits.

In the black bin, buckwheat.
And beneath the mill, bags.
The buckwheat ground between chiselled rocks.

For this corn, the perfect black stars are stoned.

The thing is named. The tailings drop.

All things
in new shape, new forms.

Dust on the floor.
Stars tied and squat.

I wait.
I listen for a sound.
A call: dark and leaning
into the shoulders of the barn.

A call: into the hand, along the arm,
into the body.

I am the rafters.
I am the sills.
I am the barn.
I am the house.

Come.

Knock
on wood. The sound is sealed
in the body
of wood; held in the grain.

Come

I am the house.

Come.

Knock on these walls.

These walls have sores.
And there is blood in the long halls.

Come.
Call for the sealed sounds of doors.

Ask
   for the sounds bound inside of barns,
   in sheds, in the beams, in the rise
   of houses, in the nests in their eaves.

Ask
   for the held call
   of windows, stairs and walls.

Break me
through the surface of things
as they seem.

Where I live only occasionally.
Making
gestures.

Where I go round as much as water goes round.

I go round as much as the light

dancing on the surface.

I go round as a child swinging out on the air
and falling back; falling upside-back.

I go round as a woman newly touched by a man
and his touch lingering on her
long after he has taken away
his hand. I go round

as a goose, as a wild bird losing its breath —
its breath taken in the wings,
kept, and not missed.

I go round when she takes my hand;
my grandmother turning me round.

We circle in this place.
We dance arm in arm.
Our hands a tight knot;
our dance a small bowl.

The boards under our feet
sound. Bones snap like lit wood.
Bones picked up and set down
when we dance. The shadows fall away

where she tosses back her dark hair
and laughs a shimmering laugh
on the surface of this place.

My grandmother pulling me round.

We have no body here; no business to keep.
We thrash our skirts and move our feet;
these are the things we speak.

We dance round. In this room, behind this glass,
within these walls.

I would have her dance forever.
It is so easy now that she is here.
I want to ask her where
she has been, how she has been —
all those things asked of a dearly awaited
and longed-for friend. But she bids me to listen
for
the
sounds.

The joints of our hands crack;
we are as timbers settling in this old house.

Our dresses sparkle into the dark
where we go round.

Two figures in a wooden place.

The grace of bodies:
hands, arms, faces.

We are a mime of being.

Face to face.
Growing round.

And hers is a silent sound
like light
like liquid.

Sound not written down but
hummed in the head.

A memory

set down in the wood,
in the grain,

resounds as toes tap and feet again
heel and toe and suddenly
she takes the concertina down
and rubs its side.

Her instrument telling me there is no end
to the room, to the stalls. To the acts of animals
looking behind for the other.

Looking the other in the eye for the world.
For the bird in the mirror
to be more than broken bones.

And someone says it's time

to be getting in.

And something leans,
dusts itself in the rafters.
Is lost in the gaping seams
of golden floors.

Some thing flutters
about my face

        soft hands
wanting

   to speak.

Some thing noses in the barn
where spittle clung, binds to the iron bit;

some thing moves, closing
doors in the still hours;

inside of houses,
  inside of barns,
    mimes of being

making gestures for themselves
they live
only occasionally
breaking through the surface of things
as they seem

For faith consists in creating what we do not see.
— Miguel de Unamuno

Acknowledgements

Versions of these poems have appeared in the following publications:

"Annabelle Hydrangea" in *The Fiddlehead*, No. 159, Spring 1989.

"Anniversary Request" in *Canadian Woman Studies*, Vol. 11, No. 1, 1990.

"The Apparition / The Field" in *The Fiddlehead*, No. 178, Winter 1993/94.

"Back Talk" in *The Pottersfield Portfolio*, Vol. 9, 1988.

"The Beginning of Sight" in *Vintage '91* (Victoria: Sono Nis Press), 1992.

"Desk-Talk" in *The Fiddlehead*, No. 159, Spring 1989.

"The Fire Place" in *The Fiddlehead*, No. 178, Winter 1993/94.

"Going Where I Touch" in *The Pottersfield Portfolio*, Vol. 13, No. 1, Spring 1991.

"Grieving his wife" in *The Pottersfield Portfolio*, Vol. 13, No. 1, Spring 1991.

"Here is the Smell of Smoke" in *The Pottersfield Portfolio*, Vol. 13, No. 1, Spring 1991.

"Image on Highway" in *The Cormorant*, Vol. 4, No. 2, 1986.

"Loon" in *Tickleace*, No. 21, Spring/Summer 1991.

"within the blood" in *Tickleace*, No. 15, Spring/Summer 1988.

"You Ask Me What I Am Afraid Of" in *The Pottersfield Portfolio*, Vol. 13, No. 1, Spring 1991.